Playtime to Bedtime Quilts

FROM

In The Beginning

SHARON EVANS YENTER

Introduction

The memories of early childhood are few and elusive. They appear in our minds as dreamlike wisps floating in a summer sky just out of our reach. Do we really remember an event, or is the memory a magical story told by a favorite grandmother?

Are recollections of scenes really true or a result of viewing family photos from years gone by, and visualizing happiness and contentment? Are memories really only a compilation of myth, daydreams, and family lore, or are they true events stored in the subconscious waiting to be discovered by a sound, smell, item, or place?

Reality is difficult to discover and the mind plays mysterious tricks when re-creating the past. Sometimes remembering childhood happiness depends on a tangible object such as a toy or a quilt. A timeworn piece can return us to the feelings of warmth and comfort we knew as babies.

Quilts are truly "security blankets" in sleep and play. A quiet afternoon nap with the familiar smells and silky touch of a favorite quilt can make us cuddle with sweet dreams. We can hide in a colorful tent or wear our quilt as a cape to make us a fearless hero or heroine.

On the opposite page, we've arranged a collection of dolls, quilts, and toys belonging to the In The Beginning staff members or their children. These are our "real" links with the past. Our lovies, bankies, silkies, honeys, quilties, raggedies, and Poohs. They remind us of this passage from *The Velveteen Rabbit*, by Margery Williams:

> *"Generally, by the time you are Real, most of your hair has been loved*
> *off and your eyes drop out and you get loose in your joints and very*
> *shabby. But these things don't matter at all, because once you are Real*
> *you can't be ugly, except to people who don't understand."*

In this book, we invite you to make a memory for a special child or cat or dog — whoever is important in your life and needs to know how much you care. These quilts are mostly easy and achieve their personalities by your choice of prints, colors, and design. Workmanship is not the most important element in your project, love is! Do the best you can and don't forget to include a dedication and signature.

Table of Contents

Basic Quiltmaking

QUILT BASICS

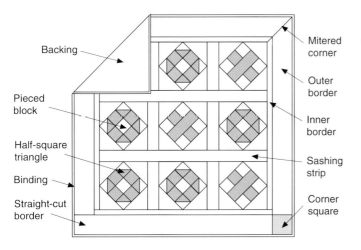

- Backing
- Pieced block
- Half-square triangle
- Binding
- Straight-cut border
- Mitered corner
- Outer border
- Inner border
- Sashing strip
- Corner square

- The **Quilt Top** often includes pieced or appliquéd blocks, sashing, and borders.
- **Batting** is the "filler," or middle layer of the quilt.
- The **Quilt Back** is usually made with a single fabric.
- **Blocks** are a main design element of many quilts.
- **Sashing** is another design element.
- **Borders** are the "frame" of the quilt, and may have straight-cut or mitered corners.
- **Binding** finishes the edges of the quilt.

BASIC SUPPLIES

- **Sewing machine.** A machine with a good straight stitch is all that's needed for piecing your quilt top. When you get to the machine-quilting stage, you'll need a walking foot (for straight-line quilting) or a darning foot (for free-motion quilting).
- **Iron and ironing board.**
- **Rotary cutter.** Pick one that fits your hand comfortably. The 45mm blade is the best size for most quilting applications.

- **Rotary mat.** You'll need one that's at least 18" x 24". If you have the space, a 24" x 36" mat is ideal.
- **Acrylic rulers** for rotary cutting. Handy sizes are 6" x 24" for cutting strips, 6" x 6" for cutting smaller pieces, and 12½" x 12½" for cutting larger pieces and squaring up blocks.
- **Scissors.**
- **Pins.**
- **Seam ripper.** It's good for ripping seams, and also helpful in steering smaller pieces of fabric through the sewing machine.
- **Tape measure.**
- **Marking tool** (optional) for marking quilting lines.
- **Stencils** (optional) for marking quilting lines.
- **Yardstick** (optional) for marking quilting lines.
- **Safety pins** for pin-basting the quilt top, batting, and backing together.

FABRIC SELECTION

All of the quilts in this book are made with high-quality 100% cotton fabric. As we designed these quilts, we tried to select many different types of prints to show the wide variety of moods that baby quilts can express. We used novelty prints designed especially for kids, 1930s and 1940s reproduction prints, floral prints, batiks, and more. Whatever type of print you choose, it's easiest to pick a focal print first, then "go-with" prints that match one or two of the colors found in the focal print. Most importantly of all, pick fabrics that make you happy, and that you think will make a baby happy. Make the quilt soft, make it cuddly, make it just his or her size, and your baby is sure to love it.

Prewashing Fabric

Once you have purchased your fabric and brought it home, we recommend prewashing it. If the fabric is going to shrink, it's best to have it shrink before it's in your quilt! Wash in warm water, with mild detergent (or no detergent, if preferred). Tumble dry on warm cycle. Press gently with a hot iron on steam setting. Take care not to stretch the fabric.

ROTARY CUTTING BASICS

If you are new to rotary cutting, practice on scrap fabric first. Always remember to:
- Keep your fingers and other body parts away from the blade (it's very sharp).
- Close the blade each time you finish cutting.
- Keep the cutter out of the reach of children.

Cutting Strips

Fold the fabric selvage to selvage, aligning the crosswise and lengthwise grains as best you can. Place fabric on the rotary cutting mat with the folded edge closest to you. Align a square plastic cutting ruler with the fold of the fabric and place a long cutting ruler to the left.

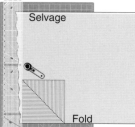

Selvage

Fold

When making all cuts, fabric should be placed to your right. (If you are left handed, reverse the directions.) Remove the square plastic cutting ruler and cut along the right side of the long ruler to trim away the uneven raw edges of fabric. Be sure to hold the long ruler firmly in place, and roll the cutter away from you, cutting through all layers.

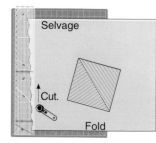

Selvage

Cut.

Fold

Make successive cuts measuring from the first cut. Refer to the quilt directions for the correct strip width. Position the ruler so that the strip width measurement (2½" for example) is aligned with the cut edge of your fabric. Cut strip.

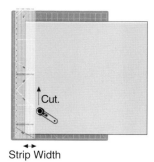

Cut.

Strip Width

Some of the quilts in this book call for lengthwise border strips. Position the fabric so cuts will be parallel to the selvage. For your first cut, evenly trim away the selvage (approximately ¾"). Refer to quilt directions for correct strip width, then make successive cuts measuring from the first cut.

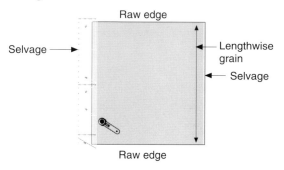

Raw edge

Selvage

Lengthwise grain

Selvage

Raw edge

Squares and Rectangles

It's easiest to cut a strip first, then to crosscut your squares or rectangles from that strip. Strips are generally cut across the width of fabric. As an example, if the quilt instructions call for 2½" squares, first cut a 2½" x 40" strip. Then position the ruler so that the square or rectangle measurement is aligned with the short cut edge of your strip. Cut through all layers.

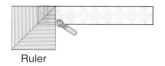

Ruler

Half-Square Triangles

Cut a square, then cut it in half diagonally once. Each of the resulting two triangles will have the short sides on the straight grain of fabric, and the long side on the bias.

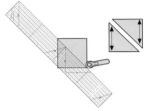

Quarter-Square Triangles

Cut a square, then cut in half diagonally twice. Each of the resulting four triangles will have the long side on the straight grain of fabric, and the short sides on the bias.

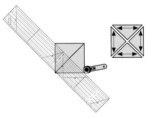

Templates

One of our quilts ("My Home is My Castle" on page 46) requires templates for four irregularly shaped triangles. With a sharp pencil, carefully trace the templates onto template plastic, then cut out. Trim off the triangle points at the marked short lines (this will make your pieces easier to match when sewing). Place templates on right side of fabric, matching arrows to straight grain of fabric. Trace around template with pencil; then cut on marked line with fabric scissors, or with rotary cutter and acrylic ruler.

Selective Cutting

Many medium- and large-scale prints have the main design elements scattered across a solid or tonal background. If you cut your fabric into strips, then cut the strips into smaller pieces as described above, the design elements might not appear exactly where you want them within your cut patches. With selective cutting, you can precisely place specific motifs. For example, in "Stars Over You" on page 20, Jackie selectively cut her floral fabric so that a rose would appear in the center of each star.

For selective cutting, trim a piece of thin template plastic to the size required. (The cutting directions will tell you the size of squares, rectangles, etc. Use these measurements when cutting your template plastic.) Mark the ¼" seam allowance on your template. Place the template over your fabric and center your chosen motif within the marked seam allowances. Try to keep your template aligned with the straight grain of the fabric. Draw around the template with a sharp pencil; then cut on marked line with fabric scissors, or with rotary cutter and acrylic ruler.

MACHINE PIECING

Use 100% cotton thread. Most quilters choose one color of thread, and use it to piece the whole quilt regardless of color changes in the fabric. If most of your prints are light to medium in value, an ecru or light gray thread is a good choice. For a predominantly dark quilt, consider dark gray, navy, or black thread.

Sew exact ¼" seams. On some machines the width of the presser foot is ¼" and can be used as a guide. If you don't have such a foot, you'll need to establish the proper seam allowance on your sewing machine. Place a piece of quarter- or eighth-inch graph paper under the presser foot and gently lower the needle onto the line that is ¼" from the edge of the paper. Lay a piece of masking tape at the edge of the paper to act as the ¼" guide.

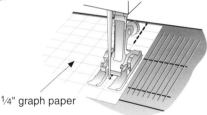

¼" graph paper

For the patterns in this book, sew from cut edge to cut edge. Backtacking is generally unnecessary.

Chain Piecing

Chain piecing is a great time-saver.

1. Sew the first set of pieces together and continue stitching off the edge for a few stitches, creating a "chain" of thread.
2. Without lifting the presser foot, arrange the next set of pieces and feed it under the foot while you sew. Continue in this manner until all of your sets have been stitched.

3. Clip the threads between the stitched units.

Masking tape guide

Pinning

Pin seams before stitching if matching is involved, or if your seams are longer than 4". Pin points of matching (where seam lines or points meet) first. Once these important points are in place, pin the rest of the seam, easing if necessary (see Easing at right).

Pressing

In this book, most seams are pressed to one side, toward the darker fabric whenever possible. Sometimes, for matching purposes, seams are pressed in opposite directions, regardless of which is the darker fabric. We sometimes press seams open to distribute bulk, as in the "Twinkling Stars" quilt on page 68.

Press with a dry iron that has a shot of steam when needed. Take care not to overpress. First, press the sewn seam flat to "set" it. Next, press the seam open or to the side as desired.

Matching

1. Opposing seams. When stitching one seamed unit to another, press seam allowances on seams that need to match in opposite directions. The two "opposing" seams will hold each other in place and evenly distribute the bulk.

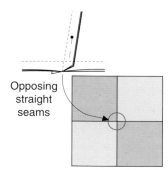

Opposing straight seams

Often, the opposing seams are diagonal seams. Plan pressing to take advantage of opposing seams.

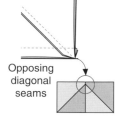

Opposing diagonal seams

2. Positioning pin. Carefully push a pin straight through two points that need to match. Pull the pin tight to establish the proper point of matching. Pin the seam normally and remove the positioning pin before stitching.

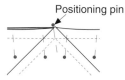

Positioning pin

3. The **X**. When triangles are pieced, stitches will form an **X** at the next seam line. Stitch through the center of the **X** to make sure the points on the sewn triangles will not be chopped off.

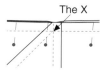

The **X**

4. Easing. When two pieces to be sewn together are supposed to match but instead are slightly different lengths, pin the points of matching and lightly steam press the seam before stitching. Stitch with the shorter piece on top. The feed dog eases the fullness of the bottom piece.

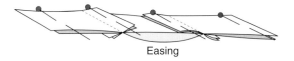

Easing

8

Setting the Quilt Blocks Together

Each quilt pattern has a Quilt Assembly Diagram showing how the blocks and setting pieces (large squares or sashing strips) will be sewn together in rows. When sewing the rows together, press for opposing seams and pin all points of matching.

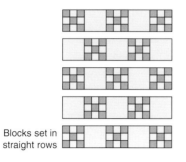

Blocks set in straight rows

Borders

The borders for most of the quilts in this book were cut and attached to the sides and then to the top and bottom edges of the quilt top. Applying borders in this order allows you to buy the least amount of fabric.

1. To cut the two side borders to the right length, measure the quilt top length (including seam allowances) through the center. Cut the two strips to this measurement. This method of measuring and cutting helps prevent waviness in your border.
2. Mark the center and quarter points on both the quilt top and border strips.
3. Matching ends, centers, and quarter points, pin border strips to the quilt top. Pin generously and press along the matched edges to set the seam before sewing. A shot of steam will help with any easing that might be required.
4. Using a ¼" seam allowance, stitch the border to the quilt top. Press the seam allowance to one side as directed in the quilt instructions.
5. Repeat steps 1-4 to measure the quilt width (including the borders just added), cut, and attach the top and bottom borders.

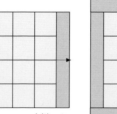

Measure length at center.

Measure width at center after adding side borders.

FINISHING YOUR QUILT

Backing

The rule of thumb for quilt backings is that they should measure 8" wider and 8" longer than your quilt top. This gives you a nice wide working margin while you do your quilting. For quilts that measure more than 37" wide, you'll need to cut your backing fabric into two lengths, which should then be sewn together along the long sides. Press seam open.

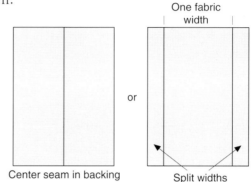

One fabric width

or

Center seam in backing

Split widths

Batting

Batting dimensions are given in the yardage requirements of each quilt pattern. In most cases, a package of crib-size batting (45" x 60") is all you'll need. If you want your quilt to have the look of vintage or antique quilts, choose a 100% cotton batting, or a 80% cotton/20% polyester batting. If you like a slightly puffier look, try a low-loft 100% polyester batting. This is an especially good choice for some of the brighter, more playful-looking quilts in the book.

Planning and Marking Quilting Designs

All of the quilts in this book were quilted by machine. Machine quilting is fast, durable, and will stand up to many washings. In other words, machine quilting is perfect for baby quilts!

Quilting lines should be evenly distributed over the quilt surface. Directions that come with your batting will tell how close the quilting lines should be to keep the batting from coming apart when the quilt is washed. Avoid tight complicated designs that then require similar quilting over the whole quilt. Likewise avoid leaving large areas unquilted.

You will need a yardstick if you plan to mark long straight quilting lines. For a variety of curved motifs, be sure to check out your local quilt shop's supply of stencils. Your choice of marking tools includes pencils, water-soluble pens, chalk pouncers, and more. No matter what kind of marking tool you choose, light lines will be easier to remove than heavy ones.

Some quilt designs don't require marking. "Stitching in the ditch" is a technique that closely follows seam lines; outline quilting is usually stitched approximately ¼" from seams, allowing you to use your machine's foot as a guide.

Layering the Quilt

1. Place the backing, face down, on a large, flat surface and smooth it out so there are no wrinkles. Use masking tape to hold it in place. The backing should be flat and slightly taut, but not stretched off grain.
2. Gently lay the batting on top of the backing, centering and smoothing it as you go.
3. Center the completed quilt top on top of the batting. Starting in the middle, gently smooth out fullness to the sides and corners. Take care not to distort the straight lines of the quilt design and the borders.
4. Use safety pins to hold the layers together, spacing them no more than a hand's width apart, or hand baste through all layers in the pattern shown, using light-colored thread (dark colors may bleed onto your quilt top when you remove them).

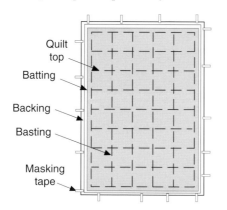

Quilting

The right sewing machine foot will make all the difference when you get ready to quilt. A walking foot is a necessity for straight-line or shallow-curve quilting. The walking foot feeds the quilt layers evenly, preventing the shifting of the backing and batting as you sew. A darning foot or similar foot is needed for the free-motion quilting of all-over curving patterns.

Machine-quilting is a huge subject. Check your quilt store or library for some of the excellent books entirely devoted to the topic. Then practice, practice, practice! And remember, babies aren't likely to criticize your quilting technique, so don't worry if your first attempt isn't perfect.

After quilting, machine-baste close to the quilt's edge, through all three layers. Trim excess batting and backing even with the edge of the quilt top. A rotary cutter and long acrylic ruler will ensure accurate straight edges.

Binding

Binding is the final step in finishing your quilt. The quilts in this book are bound with either straight grain or bias binding. Both methods are given below. The fabric requirements given for each quilt are enough to make either type of binding, so always feel free to substitute your preferred technique.

Straight Grain Binding:

Cut binding strips 2½" wide, across the width of fabric (approximately 40" wide). Join the strips together using diagonal seams as shown. Make enough continuous binding to go around the four sides of the quilt plus 6" to 10" for overlap.

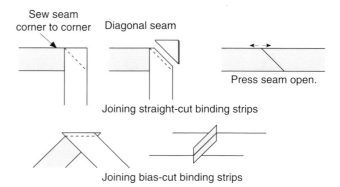

Continuous Bias Binding:

A ½ yd. piece of fabric, cut into two 18" squares, will make approximately 240" of continuous bias binding, enough to finish any of the quilts in this book.

1. Begin with an 18" square of fabric. Fold diagonally and press. Cut on the diagonal line.

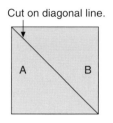

Cut on diagonal line.

2. With right sides together, and sides A and B matching, stitch the two triangles together and press the seam open.

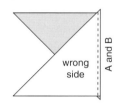

3. Draw pencil lines 2½" apart, on the wrong side of the fabric, as shown. These will be your cutting lines.

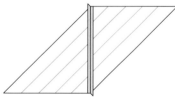

4. With right sides together, align edge of fabric with first pencil line as shown. Match remaining pencil lines and pin, creating a lopsided tube. Sew the seam and press open. Cut around the tube on the pencil lines for yards of continuous bias.

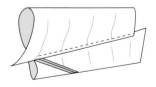

Applying Binding to Quilt

1. Fold the binding in half lengthwise with wrong sides together and press, taking care not to stretch it. At one end, open out the fold and turn the raw edge in at a 45° angle. Press. Trim, leaving a ¼" seam allowance.

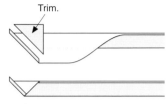

Trim.

2. Beginning on one edge of the quilt a few inches from a corner, pin the binding to the quilt top. Beginning two inches from the folded end of the binding, stitch ⅜" from the raw edges and stop ⅜" from the raw edge at the corner. Backstitch and remove the quilt.

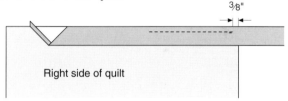

⅜"

Right side of quilt

3. Fold the binding back on itself to create a 45° angle, then turn the binding down to make a fold in the binding that is in line with the upper raw edge of the quilt top. Pin. Stitch the binding to the quilt, ending ⅜" from the next corner. Backstitch and miter the corner as you did the previous one.

Fold.   Fold.

4. Continue in this manner until the binding has been stitched to all four edges of the quilt top. When you reach the beginning of the binding, trim away excess, leaving 1" to tuck into the folded binding. Complete the stitching.

5. Turn the binding to the back of the quilt and hand sew in place, mitering corners as shown.

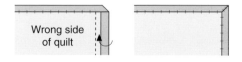

Wrong side
of quilt

Pretty Baby

Jackie made this quilt for her newest grandchild, baby Chloe, and selected elements of the quilt to represent Chloe's parents. The Irish Chain pattern honors the heritage of dad, Charlie: Irish by way of Seattle, USA. The beautiful toile fabric in the border honors the heritage of mom, Nancy: French by way of Paris, France. The couple met in New York and now make their home in Brooklyn. The fabric and pattern combine to make a beautiful and meaningful quilt so little Chloe can remember Grandma Jackie back in the Pacific Northwest.

When you make a special quilt, be sure to record the child's name and birthdate on the label, as well as your own name and location. Consider adding a dedication, perhaps a little poem or wish, so that the recipient of the quilt will know the added meaning you have sewn into his or her gift.

Photo-transfer supplies, which are readily available, allow you to include a picture of yourself on the label, or you might use a birth picture of baby and sew on the label later.

Jackie's friend, Ruby, enjoys playtime with Chloe's quilt before it's carefully packaged and mailed to Chloe in New York.

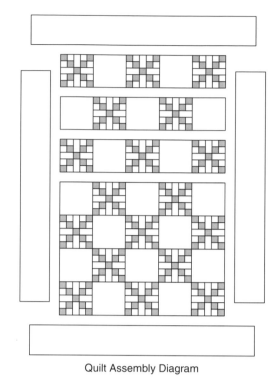

Quilt Assembly Diagram

Pretty Baby

DESIGNED BY:
Jackie Quinn

QUILTED BY:
Kathy Staley

Finished quilt size:
43¾" x 56¼"

Finished block size:
6¼" x 6¼"

MATERIALS

Fabric requirements are based on 40" fabric width.

	Yardage	Cut
1¾ yds.*	Floral bouquet on white background for alternate squares	17 squares, 6¾" x 6¾"
⅞ yd.	Small floral print on white background for Irish Chain blocks	7 strips, 1¾" x 40" 2 strips, 3" x 40" 36 rectangles, 1¾" x 3"
½ yd.	Pink tone-on-tone for Irish Chain blocks	8 strips, 1¾" x 40"
2½ yds.	Pink toile for border and binding	*Instructions are for one-directional print. Cut pieces in order given.* 6 widthwise binding strips, 2½" x 40" 3 widthwise border strips, 6½" x 40" 2 lengthwise border strips, 6½" x 46"**
4 yds.	Backing	
48" x 61"	Batting	

* Yardage is generous to allow for selective cutting of floral motifs.

** Strips are cut longer than necessary, and will be trimmed to size later.

DIRECTIONS

See *Basic Quiltmaking,* beginning on page 5, for general quiltmaking directions.

Block Assembly

1. Using 7 small floral 1¾" strips and 7 pink tone-on-tone 1¾" strips, make 7 strip units as shown. Press seams toward pink strip. From the strip units, cut 144 segments, each 1¾" wide.

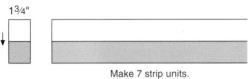

1¾"

Make 7 strip units.
Cut 144 segments.

2. Arrange the segments in pairs and sew together to make 72 Fourpatch units. Press seams in one direction.

Make 72.

3. Using 2 small floral 3" strips and 1 pink tone-on-tone 1¾" strip, make 1 strip unit as shown. Press seams toward small floral strips. From the strip units, cut 18 segments, each 1¾" wide.

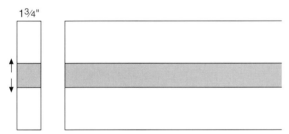

1¾"

Make 1 strip unit.
Cut 18 segments.

4. Using Fourpatch units, segments from Step 3, and small floral rectangles, assemble Irish Chain block as shown. Press seams in direction of arrows.

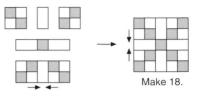

Make 18.

5. Sew Irish Chain blocks and alternate squares together in horizontal rows. Press seams toward alternate squares. Sew rows together as shown in the Quilt Assembly Diagram on page 14.

Border

1. Measure length of quilt top through center. Trim 2 lengthwise border strips to this measurement, and sew to sides of quilt. Press seams toward border.

2. Sew the 3 widthwise border strips together, end-to-end. Measure width of quilt top, including borders just added, through center. From the long border strip, cut 2 strips to this measurement, and sew to top and bottom of quilt. Press seams toward border.

Finishing

1. Cut the backing fabric into two equal lengths and sew long edges together. Press seam open. Trim backing to 52" x 65".
2. Plan and mark quilting design as desired.
3. Layer quilt top, batting, and backing. Baste layers together.
4. Quilt by hand or machine.
5. Trim the batting and backing even with the quilt top edges.
6. Sew the binding strips together to create one long strip. Bind the quilt edges.
7. Add a hanging sleeve if desired. Sign and date your finished quilt.

Lecko My Gecko!

Where can three lucky kids stay up just a little bit past their bedtime? Try on a collection of sparkling hats and tiaras? Dance barefoot in the kitchen with the radio turned up loud? Stage a puppet show? At Grandma Doodle's house, that's where. Trish's three grandchildren know that their Doodle is a kindred spirit. She supplies love, understanding, and when bedtime finally comes, quilts.

Trish picked the bright gecko print for the focal fabric of her quilt, but her design would work equally well with any of the novelty prints currently available.

Vibrant colors, fun prints, and bold block designs are perfect choices for children's quilts. Novelty prints also give quilters a chance to cut loose and play. Most of us are accustomed to making "adult" quilts, with every fabric choice carefully considered. Trish is a mentor to many of her coworkers, who admire her go-for-it attitude, and her fearless use of the bright, brighter, and brightest prints.

Granddaughter Kelsey and friend Dylan practice their marionette skills in an impromptu show before bedtime.

Quilt Assembly Diagram

Lecko My Gecko!

DESIGNED BY:
Trish Carey

QUILTED BY:
Kathy Staley

Finished quilt size:
41" x 41"

Finished block size:
10½" x 10½"

MATERIALS

Fabric requirements are based on 40" fabric width.

	Yardage	Cut
1⅓ yds.	Focal print for block centers and border	*Cut pieces in order given.* 2 lengthwise border strips, 5" x 43"* 2 lengthwise border strips, 5" x 34"* 9 squares, 5" x 5" (5 for A Blocks, 4 for B Blocks)
¼ yd. *each*	Green, orange, lavender, and yellow tone-on-tone prints for blocks	*From each color, cut:* 5 rectangles, 1½" x 5" (A Block) 4 rectangles, 2½" x 7" (B Block)
¾ yd.	Rainbow stripe for blocks and binding	*Cut pieces in order given.* 2 squares, 18" x 18", to use for continuous bias binding (see page 11) 20 squares, 1½" x 1½" (A Block) 16 squares, 2½" x 2½" (B Block)
¼ yd.	Bright print for blocks	20 squares, 2½" x 2½" (A Block) 16 squares, 1½" x 1½" (B Block)
½ yd.	Black-and-white print for blocks	20 rectangles, 2½" x 7" (A Block)
¼ yd.	Black-and-white check for blocks	16 rectangles, 1½" x 5" (B Block)
3 yds.	Backing	
45" x 45"	Batting	

* Strips are cut longer than necessary, and will be trimmed to size later.

DIRECTIONS

See *Basic Quiltmaking,* beginning on page 5, for general quiltmaking directions.

Block Assembly

Before starting to sew, separate all the squares and rectangles into two groups as designated in the cutting instructions: one group for A Blocks, and one for B Blocks. A and B Blocks are assembled the same, but pay particular attention to the pressing instructions. The blocks are pressed differently to allow for opposing seams. Also, refer to photograph on page 17 for proper placement of the tone-on-tone prints.

1. Using all of your A Block pieces, assemble 5 blocks as shown. Press seams in direction of arrows.

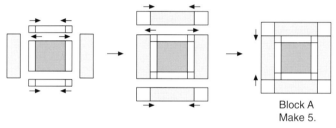

Block A
Make 5.

2. Using all of your B Block pieces, assemble 4 blocks as shown. Press seams in direction of arrows.

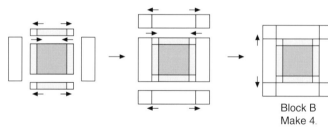

Block B
Make 4.

3. Sew blocks in horizontal rows (A Blocks should be in corners and center of quilt); then sew rows together as shown in the Quilt Assembly Diagram on page 18. Press for opposing seams (see page 8).

Border

1. Measure length of quilt top through center. Trim the 34" border strips to this measurement, and sew to sides of quilt. Press seams toward border.
2. Measure width of quilt top, including borders just added, through center. Trim the 43" border strips to this measurement, and sew to top and bottom of quilt. Press seams toward border.

Finishing

1. Cut the backing fabric into two equal lengths and sew long edges together. Press seam open. Trim backing to 49" x 49".
2. Plan and mark quilting design as desired.
3. Layer quilt top, batting, and backing. Baste layers together.
4. Quilt by hand or machine.
5. Trim the batting and backing even with the quilt top edges.
6. Bind the quilt edges with continuous bias binding (see page 11).
7. Add a hanging sleeve if desired. Sign and date your finished quilt.

Stars Over You

Jackie says that since this quilt has 35 stars, she's saving it for her 35th grandchild. For first-time grandmothers, this might seem like an extreme statement, but with 17 grandchildren already, she is well on her way to fulfilling her promise! (Confidentially, we have the feeling that Jackie is very fond of this quilt and created 35 stars to insure that the quilt remains in her possession.)

Jackie chose soft and pretty pastel colors for "Stars Over You." To make sure that a flower showed up in the center square of each star, she selectively cut her focal fabric. (See page 7 for technique.) The result is a quietly romantic blanket of stars.

What is more fun than a tea party on a warm spring afternoon? A starry garland in her hair makes a young girl feel like a princess, and friendships bloom in the presence of tea, ice cream, and cakes. Aleyah, Kimberly, and Fiona visit and laugh in front of a beautiful quilt, which adds charm and elegance to their special event.

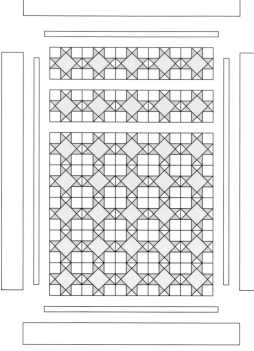

Quilt Assembly Diagram

Stars Over You

DESIGNED BY:
Jackie Quinn

QUILTED BY:
Kathy Staley

Finished quilt size:
40½" x 52½"

Finished block size:
6" x 6"

MATERIALS

Fabric requirements are based on 40" fabric width.

	Yardage	Cut
¾ yd.*	Large floral with blue background for star centers	35 squares, 3⅜" x 3⅜"
¾ yd.	Small floral with blue background for star points	70 squares, 3¼" x 3¼"; cut each square twice diagonally to make 280 star-point triangles
1⅛ yds.	Light print for block background	140 squares, 2½" x 2½" 35 squares, 3¼" x 3¼"; cut each square twice diagonally to make 140 background triangles
⅓ yd.	Pink tone-on-tone for inner border	5 strips, 1½" x 40"
2 yds.	Blue/beige print for outer border and binding	*Cut pieces in order given.* 6 widthwise binding strips, 2½" x 40" 4 lengthwise border strips, 4½" x 46"**
3½ yds.	Backing	
44½" x 56½"	Batting	

* Yardage is generous to allow for selective cutting of floral motifs.

** Strips are cut longer than necessary, and will be trimmed to size later.

DIRECTIONS

See *Basic Quiltmaking*, beginning on page 5, for general quiltmaking directions.

Block Assembly

1. Sew 2 star-point triangles to a 2½" background square as shown. Press seams toward triangles.

Make 140.

2. Using units made in Step 1, background triangles, and 3⅜" squares, assemble Star blocks as shown. Press seams in direction of arrows.

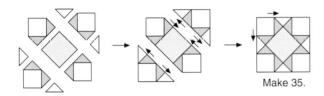

Make 35.

3. Sew blocks together in horizontal rows, then join rows together as shown in the Quilt Assembly Diagram on page 22. Press seams open to reduce bulk.

Borders

1. Sew 3 of the pink border strips together, end-to-end, to make one long strip. Measure length of quilt top through center. From the long strip, cut 2 strips to this measurement, and sew to sides of quilt. Press seams toward border.

2. Measure width of quilt top, including borders just added, through center. Trim the remaining 2 pink border strips to this measurement, and sew to top and bottom of quilt. Press seams toward border.

3. Following general instructions in Steps 1 and 2 above, measure, trim, and sew blue/beige border strips. Add side borders first, then top and bottom borders. Press seams toward border.

Finishing

1. Cut the backing fabric into two equal lengths and sew long edges together. Press seam open. Trim backing to 48½" x 60½".
2. Plan and mark quilting design as desired.
3. Layer quilt top, batting, and backing. Baste layers together.
4. Quilt by hand or machine.
5. Trim the batting and backing even with the quilt top edges.
6. Sew the binding strips together to create one long strip. Bind the quilt edges.
7. Add a hanging sleeve if desired. Sign and date your finished quilt.

Tic-Tac-Toby

Many of the events in our lives are serendipitous and out of our control, but we know somehow they are meant to be. We think we have everything and then a baby or pet comes into our life and we wonder how we lived without them. Such is the story of Wendy and her husband Tom. One night they were greeted at their front steps by a young, handsome, gray cat who clearly wanted to go inside.

He had no collar and didn't respond to kindly-meant commands to "go home!" Closer inspection revealed a nasty wound on his haunch. The next morning, a veterinarian examined the cat and listened as Wendy talked optimistically about finding his family.

"He's nice, but we're really not looking for another cat," she said.

"Don't name him then," the vet warned.

"Toby," Wendy instantly responded, "He's a perfect Toby!"

Toby now makes his home with Wendy, Tom, and their two other very special cats. As she chose fabric for her quilt, the cats in the focal print reminded her of Toby's jaunty, self-assured attitude, and "Tic-Tac-Toby" was born.

Why settle for one quilt when you can lounge on a whole stack of them? With his own quilt hanging behind him, Toby clearly believes that "more is more."

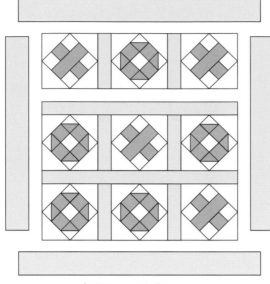

Quilt Assembly Diagram

Tic-Tac-Toby

DESIGNED BY:
Wendy Slotboom

QUILTED BY:
Wendy Slotboom

Finished quilt size:
40" x 40"

Finished block size:
8½" x 8½"

MATERIALS

Fabric requirements are based on 40" fabric width.

	Yardage	Cut
⅝ yd.	Blue/black print for Xs and Os	3 strips, 2½" x 22" 4 rectangles, 2½" x 6½" 10 squares, 2⅞" x 2⅞" 10 squares, 2½" x 2½"
½ yd.	Orange tone-on-tone for background of X blocks	8 squares, 5⅛" x 5⅛"; cut each square once diagonally to make 16 triangles 2 strips, 2½" x 22"
½ yd.	Green tone-on-tone for background of O blocks	10 squares, 5⅛" x 5⅛"; cut each square once diagonally to make 20 triangles 1 strip, 2½" x 22" 10 squares, 2⅞" x 2⅞"
1¾ yds.	Multicolor print for sashing and border	*Instructions are for one-directional print. Cut pieces in order given.* 2 widthwise border strips, 5½" x 40½"* 2 widthwise sashing strips, 2½" x 30" 2 lengthwise border strips, 5½" x 30" 6 lengthwise sashing strips, 2½" x 9"
½ yd.	Blue tone-on-tone for binding	5 strips, 2½" x 40"
3 yds.	Backing	
44" x 44"	Batting	

* Most 44-45" fabric, after prewashing, will still be wide enough to cut a 40½" strip. If your fabric doesn't allow a 40½" strip, you will need to cut three border strips (rather than two). Sew together the three strips, end-to-end, and from this long strip, cut two strips, each 40½". Yardage allows for extra strip.

DIRECTIONS

See *Basic Quiltmaking*, beginning on page 5, for general quiltmaking directions.

Block Assembly

"X" Blocks

1. Using 1 blue/black strip and 2 orange tone-on-tone strips, make 1 strip unit as shown. Press seams toward blue/black strip. From the strip unit, cut 8 segments, each 2½" wide.

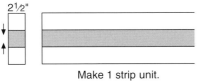

Make 1 strip unit.
Cut 8 segments.

2. Sew together 2 blue/black/orange segments and 1 blue/black rectangle as shown. Press seams toward rectangle.

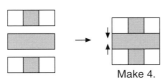

Make 4.

3. Add 4 orange tone-on-tone triangles to block. Press seams toward triangles.

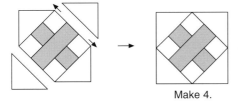

Make 4.

"O" Blocks

1. Using 1 green tone-on-tone strip and 2 blue/black strips, make 1 strip unit as shown. Press seams toward blue/black strips. From the strip unit, cut 5 segments, each 2½" wide.

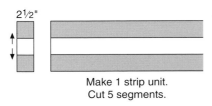

Make 1 strip unit.
Cut 5 segments.

2. Using a ruler and sharp pencil, draw a diagonal line, from corner to corner, on the wrong side of the green tone-on-tone 2⅞" squares.

3. With right sides together, place a green tone-on-tone square on top of a blue/black 2⅞" square. Sew ¼" on each side of drawn line. Cut on drawn line. Open squares and press seams toward blue/black fabric.

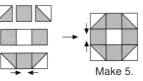

Make 20.

4. Sew together blue/black/green segments, triangle units, and 2½" blue/black squares as shown. Press seams in direction of arrows.

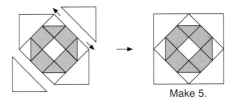

Make 5.

5. Add 4 green tone-on-tone triangles to block. Press seams toward triangles.

Make 5.

Sashing and Border

1. Sew together blocks and sashing strips as shown in the Quilt Assembly Diagram on page 26. (First, join blocks and short sashing strips into horizontal rows; then sew together rows and long sashing strips.) Press seams toward sashing strips.

2. Sew the 5½" x 30" border strips to sides of quilt top. Press seams toward border.

3. Sew the 5½" x 40½" border strips to top and bottom of quilt. Press seams toward border.

Finishing

1. Cut the backing fabric into two equal lengths and sew long edges together. Press seam open. Trim backing to 48" x 48".

2. Plan and mark quilting design as desired.

3. Layer quilt top, batting, and backing. Baste layers together.

4. Quilt by hand or machine.

5. Trim the batting and backing even with the quilt top edges.

6. Sew the binding strips together to create one long strip. Bind the quilt edges.

7. Add a hanging sleeve if desired. Sign and date your finished quilt.

In the Garden

Trish is an avid gardener who especially loves the look of English gardens. She tries to get that look in her own yard, but she admits the results aren't always what she had in mind! Still, Trish's garden is filled with flowers and other growing things (grandchildren, a cat or two, a visiting dog). In other words, it's beautiful!

As a quilter who loves gardens, Trish naturally has a keen eye for floral fabrics. For "In the Garden," she chose a rose print as her focal fabric, then designed a bird's eye view of her fantasy backyard. The pale green rectangles represent hedges. Follow the pink stepping stones from one garden "room" to another. Imagine the sage green squares as trimmed shrubs. And everywhere you look, flowers.

This makes an ultra pretty, feminine quilt for a little girl. Teach them early that a garden can bloom out of dirt or out of fabric!

Emily thinks Trish's quilt is the perfect backdrop for her piano recital in front of family and friends. Are the flowers and tiara a clue that this little cutie might be thinking of a future run at the Miss America title? Watch for her in 2020!

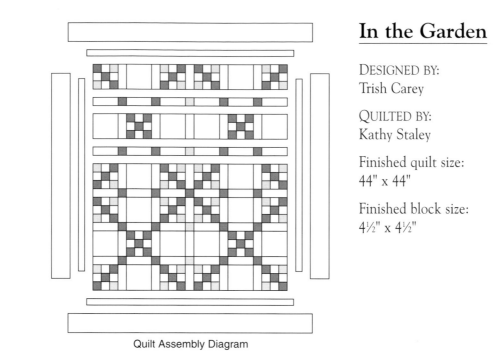

Quilt Assembly Diagram

In the Garden

DESIGNED BY:
Trish Carey

QUILTED BY:
Kathy Staley

Finished quilt size:
44" x 44"

Finished block size:
4½" x 4½"

MATERIALS

Fabric requirements are based on 40" fabric width.

	Yardage	Cut
1⅞ yds.	Large floral print for alternate blocks, outer border, and binding	*Cut pieces in order given.* 5 widthwise binding strips, 2½" x 40" 4 lengthwise border strips, 4" x 46"* 16 squares, 5" x 5"
¾ yd.	Pink tone-on-tone for ninepatch blocks, cornerstones, and inner border	5 strips, 2" x 40" 21 cornerstone squares, 2" x 2" 4 border strips, 1½" x 40"*
⅔ yd.	Sage green stripe for sashing	60 rectangles, 2" x 5"
½ yd.	Small floral on beige background for ninepatch blocks	5 strips, 2" x 40"
¼ yd.	Small floral on sage green background for ninepatch blocks and cornerstones	2 strips, 2" x 40" 4 cornerstone squares, 2" x 2"
3⅛ yds.	Backing	
48" x 48"	Batting	

* Strips are cut longer than necessary, and will be trimmed to size later.

DIRECTIONS

See *Basic Quiltmaking*, beginning on page 5, for general quiltmaking directions.

Block Assembly

1. Using 2 pink tone-on-tone strips, 2 small floral on beige strips, and 2 small floral on sage strips (all 2" x 40"), make 2 strip units as shown. Press seams toward outer strips. From the strip units cut 32 segments, each 2" wide.

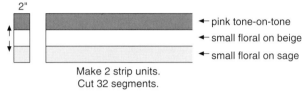

2"

← pink tone-on-tone
← small floral on beige
← small floral on sage

Make 2 strip units.
Cut 32 segments.

2. Using 2 small floral on beige strips, and 1 pink tone-on-tone strip, make 1 strip unit as shown. Press seams toward pink strip. From the strip unit, cut 20 segments, each 2" wide.

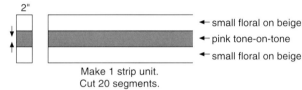

2"

← small floral on beige
← pink tone-on-tone
← small floral on beige

Make 1 strip unit.
Cut 20 segments.

3. Using 2 pink tone-on-tone strips, and 1 small floral on beige strip, make 1 strip unit as shown. Press seams toward pink strips. From the strip unit, cut 8 segments, each 2" wide.

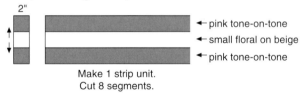

2"

← pink tone-on-tone
← small floral on beige
← pink tone-on-tone

Make 1 strip unit.
Cut 8 segments.

4. Using 32 segments from Step 1, and 16 segments from Step 2, make 16 Ninepatch A blocks as shown. Press seams in direction of arrows.

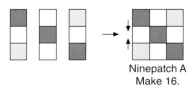

Ninepatch A
Make 16.

5. Using 8 segments from Step 3, and 4 segments from Step 2, make 4 Ninepatch B blocks as shown. Press seams in direction of arrows.

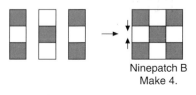

Ninepatch B
Make 4.

Sashing

1. Referring to the Quilt Assembly Diagram on page 30 and the photograph on page 29, make 5 long sashing strips using 30 sage stripe rectangles, 21 pink cornerstone squares, and 4 sage cornerstone squares. Press seams toward sage stripe rectangles.

2. Sew 5" floral squares, Ninepatch A and Ninepatch B blocks, and remaining sage stripe rectangles together in horizontal rows as shown in the Quilt Assembly Diagram. Refer again to the photograph to make sure of proper placement of the Ninepatch A and Ninepatch B blocks. Press seams toward sage stripe rectangles. Join rows and long sashing strips together. Press seams toward sashing strips.

Borders

1. Measure length of quilt top through center. Trim 2 of the pink border strips to this measurement, and sew to sides of quilt. Press seams toward border.

2. Measure width of quilt top, including borders just added, through center. Trim the remaining 2 pink border strips to this measurement, and sew to top and bottom of quilt. Press seams toward border.

3. Following general instructions in Steps 1 and 2 above, measure, trim, and sew floral border strips. Add side borders first, then top and bottom borders. Press seams toward border.

Finishing

1. Cut the backing fabric into two equal lengths and sew long edges together. Press seam open. Trim backing to 52" x 52".

2. Plan and mark quilting design as desired.

3. Layer quilt top, batting, and backing. Baste layers together.

4. Quilt by hand or machine.

5. Trim the batting and backing even with the quilt top edges.

6. Sew the binding strips together to create one long strip. Bind the quilt edges.

7. Add a hanging sleeve if desired. Sign and date your finished quilt.

Going to Ruthie's House

We know Leah for her sense of fun and adventurous spirit. Leah started her journeys one day, at the age of four, when she decided she wanted to go to her friend Ruthie's house.

With two little friends in tow, Leah asked her mother for a ride to Ruthie's. Her busy mom, Ann, gently refused. Leah responded, "Then we'll run away!"

Thinking the back yard fence was secure and knowing the journey was a three-mile round trip, Ann said, "Would you like me to fix you a lunch?" Leah said no, and left in a four-year-old's huff.

A short time later, Ann realized the little group was missing and frantically called Leah's dad, Dean. After a couple hours of searching, he spotted Leah and her friends about a block from home. When he inquired where she'd been, Leah replied, "Ruthie's house, but no one was home."

Her parents stared at her in disbelief, but her story was corroborated later that evening when Ruthie's mom called to report she had found Leah's sweater on their front porch.

After retrieving the sweater and delivering a short lecture on the dangers of "running away," Ann's first gray hair appeared on her head. Happily, Leah didn't run away from home again until 23 years later when she married husband Mike.

Leah's daughter Jennifer has no intention of leaving home. A car ride to Grandma's house is her idea of an exciting getaway for a special weekend!

MATERIALS

Fabric requirements are based on 40" fabric width.

	Yardage	Cut
¼ yd.	Yellow print #1 for roofs	5 Piece D, 3½" x 8½"
¾ yds.	Yellow print #2 for doors, Stepping Stone blocks, and outer border	*Cut pieces in order given.* 4 border strips, 4½" x 40"* 5 Piece K, 3½" x 1½" 4 squares, 2½" x 2½"
⅛ yd.	Yellow print #3 for windows	1 strip H, 1¼" x 40"
⅛ yd.	Blue print #1 for windows	1 strip H, 1¼" x 40"
1 yd.	Blue print #2 for House block background, Stepping Stone blocks, and sashing	10 Piece A, 1½" x 4" 10 Piece C, 3½" x 3½" 10 Piece E, 4½" x 1" 16 rectangles, 1½" x 2½" 16 rectangles, 1½" x 4½" 16 rectangles, 1½" x 6½" 24 sashing strips, 1½" x 8½"
⅛ yd. *each*	Five different red, white, and blue prints for house siding	*For each house cut:* 1 Piece F, 1½" x 7½" 2 Piece G, 3½" x 1" 2 Piece I, 3½" x 1½" 2 Piece J, 2" x 2"
⅔ yd.	Red/white check for chimneys, Stepping Stones blocks, cornerstones, and binding	5 Piece B, 1½" x 1½" 64 squares, 1½" x 1½" 5 binding strips, 2½" x 40"
¼ yd.	Red print for inner border	4 border strips, 1½" x 32"*
2¾ yds.**	Backing	
42½" x 42½"	Batting	

House Block

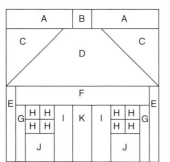

* Strips are cut longer than necessary, and will be trimmed to size later.

** If you don't mind working with a smaller-than-usual margin of backing fabric in your "quilt sandwich," it's possible to get the backing out of one length (rather than two) of 44-45"-wide fabric. In that case, you'll need 1⅜ yds. backing fabric.

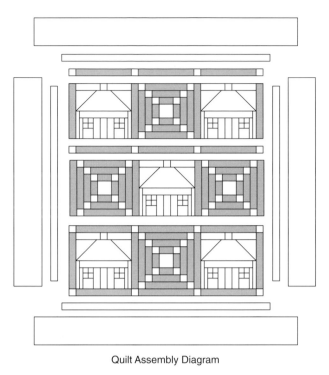

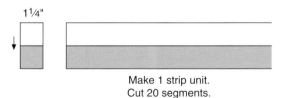

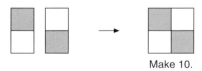

Quilt Assembly Diagram

Going to Ruthie's House

DESIGNED BY:
Leah Nelson

QUILTED BY:
Leah Nelson

Finished quilt size:
38½" x 38½"

Finished block size:
8" x 8"

DIRECTIONS

See *Basic Quiltmaking*, beginning on page 5, for general quiltmaking directions.

House Block Assembly

1. Using the yellow print #3 strip and blue print #1 strip, make a strip unit as shown. Press seam toward blue strip. From the strip unit, cut 20 segments, each 1¼" wide.

1¼"

Make 1 strip unit.
Cut 20 segments.

2. Arrange the segments in pairs and sew together to make 10 windows.

Make 10.

3. Using a ruler and sharp pencil, draw a diagonal line, from corner to corner, on the wrong side of all the Piece C squares.

4. With right sides together, place 2 Piece C squares on top of a Piece D rectangle. Sew on drawn lines. Trim as shown, leaving a ¼" seam allowance. Press seams toward triangles.

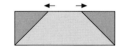

Make 5.

5. Assemble house pieces in rows as shown. Then sew rows together. Press seams in direction of arrows.

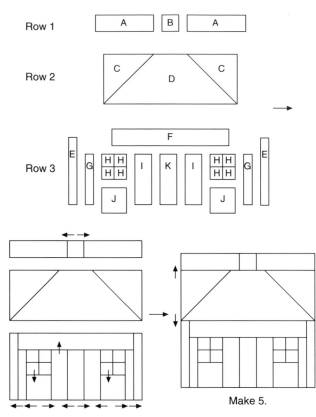

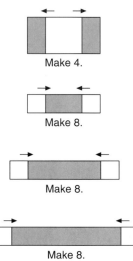

Make 5.

Stepping Stone Block Assembly

1. Using 4 yellow print #2 squares; the following blue print #2 rectangles: 16 (1½" x 2½"), 8 (1½" x 4½"), 8 (1½" x 6½"); and 48 red/white check squares, assemble Stepping Stone pieces into segments as shown. Press seams in direction of arrows.

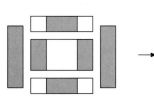

Make 4.

Make 8.

Make 8.

Make 8.

2. Using segments from Step 1 and remaining blue print #2 rectangles, assemble 4 Stepping Stone blocks as shown.

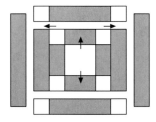

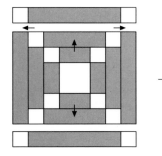

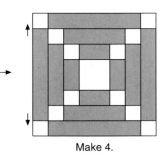

Make 4.

Sashing

1. Make 4 long strips using 12 blue print #2 sashing strips and 16 red/white check cornerstones as shown in the Quilt Assembly Diagram on page 35. Press seams toward sashing strips.

2. Sew blocks and remaining 12 blue print #2 sashing strips together in horizontal rows. Press seams toward sashing strips. Join rows and long sashing strips together. Press seams toward sashing strips.

Borders

1. Measure length of quilt top through center. Trim 2 of the red border strips to this measurement, and sew to sides of quilt. Press seams toward border.

2. Measure width of quilt top, including borders just added, through center. Trim the remaining 2 red border strips to this measurement, and sew to top and bottom of quilt. Press seams toward border.

3. Following general instructions in Steps 1 and 2 above, measure, trim, and sew yellow print #2 border strips. Add side borders first, then top and bottom borders. Press seams toward border.

Finishing

1. Cut the backing fabric into two equal lengths and sew long edges together. Press seam open. Trim backing to 46½" x 46½".

2. Plan and mark quilting design as desired.

3. Layer quilt top, batting, and backing. Baste layers together.

4. Quilt by hand or machine.

5. Trim the batting and backing even with the quilt top edges.

6. Sew the binding strips together to create one long strip. Bind the quilt edges.

7. Add a hanging sleeve if desired. Sign and date your finished quilt.

I Love a Parade

Kristine loves her new role as grandma to her first grandchild, Cassandra Rose. She made a pinwheel basket quilt for Cassie, then, with inspiration still flowing, made "I Love a Parade" in eye-catching black and white prints. Kristine picked flannel fabrics to make sure her quilt would be soft, cuddly, and the perfect "blankie" for Cassie to drag to her first parade!

Remember the small town parades on the 4th of July? The firetruck was the star, followed closely by the ambulance, the mayor's car, utility trucks, the high school marching band, assorted kids and grown-ups in flamboyant finery, and a colorful helicopter. (Our town was lucky to have this last exotic piece of equipment!)

Be sure to include special events, stories, and pictures of baby's hometown at the time of his or her birth with your quilt gift. Sign and date your quilt and enclosure so baby remembers you!

Cassie, surrounded by her grandmother's quilt and her great grandmother's and great grandfather's vintage teddy bears, seems to be saying, "I've got the flag and the firetruck, where's the parade?"

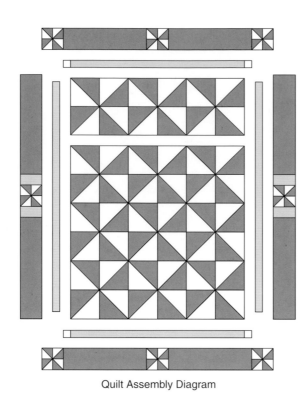

Quilt Assembly Diagram

I Love a Parade

DESIGNED BY:
Kristine Kerschner

QUILTED BY:
Kristine Kerschner

Finished quilt size:
38½" x 48½"

Finished block size:
10" x 10"

MATERIALS

Fabric requirements are based on 40" fabric width.

	Yardage	Cut
½ yd. *each*	Three different black and white prints (predominantly black) for blocks	24 squares, 5⅞" x 5⅞" 16 squares, 2⅜" x 2⅜"
½ yd. *each*	Three different black and white prints (predominantly white) for blocks	24 squares, 5⅞" x 5⅞" 16 squares, 2⅜" x 2⅜" 4 cornerstone squares, 1½" x 1½"
⅝ yd.	Black and white print (predominantly black) for outer border	4 rectangles, 3½" x 15" 4 rectangles, 3½" x 18½"
⅜ yd.	Solid red for inner border and outer border accent	2 strips, 1½" x 30½" 2 strips, 1½" x 40½"* 4 rectangles, 3½" x 2"
⅝ yd.	Black/red plaid for binding	2 squares, 18" x 18", to use for continuous bias binding (see page 11)
3⅓ yds.	Backing	
42½" x 52½"	Batting	

* Most 44-45" fabric, after prewashing, will still be wide enough to cut a 40½" strip. If your fabric doesn't allow a 40½" strip, you will need to cut three strips (rather than two). Sew together the three strips, end-to-end, and from this long strip, cut two strips, each 40½". Yardage allows for extra strip.

DIRECTIONS

See *Basic Quiltmaking*, beginning on page 5, for general quiltmaking directions.

Block Assembly

1. Using a ruler and sharp pencil, draw a diagonal line, from corner to corner, on the wrong side of all the predominantly white squares (5⅞" and 2⅜").

2. With right sides together, place a predominantly white square on top of a like-sized predominantly black square. Sew ¼" on each side of drawn line. Cut on drawn line. Open squares and press seams toward darker fabric.

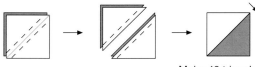

Make 48 triangle units for large pinwheels, and 32 triangle units for small pinwheels.

3. Sew like-sized triangle units together to make Pinwheel blocks as shown. Press seams open to reduce bulk.

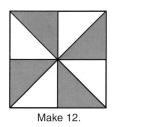

Make 12.

Make 8.

4. Sew blocks together in horizontal rows, then join rows together as shown in the Quilt Assembly Diagram on page 40. Press seams open to reduce bulk.

Borders

1. For inner border, sew cornerstone squares to opposite ends of each 1½" x 30½" red border strip. Press seams toward border strips. Sew 1½" x 40½" red border strips to sides of quilt top. Press seams toward border. Sew red strips with cornerstones to top and bottom of quilt. Press seams toward border.

2. For each outer side border, sew together 1 small pinwheel block, two 3½" x 2" red rectangles, and two 3½" x 18½" rectangles. Press seams toward red rectangles. Sew borders to sides of quilt. Press seams toward borders.

3. For each top and bottom border, sew together 3 small pinwheel blocks, and two 3½" x 15" rectangles. Press seams toward rectangles. Sew borders to top and bottom of quilt. Press seams toward border.

Finishing

1. Cut the backing fabric into two equal lengths and sew long edges together. Press seam open. Trim backing to 46½" x 56½".

2. Plan and mark quilting design as desired.

3. Layer quilt top, batting, and backing. Baste layers together.

4. Quilt by hand or machine.

5. Trim the batting and backing even with the quilt top edges.

6. Bind the quilt edges with continuous bias binding (see page 11).

7. Add a hanging sleeve if desired. Sign and date your finished quilt.

Hugs and Kisses

The popularity of French toiles combined with large florals inspired Jackie to create this decidedly feminine flannel quilt. Jackie remembered the soft feel of satin against her face in a "long-ago" quilt from her childhood, and trimmed "Hugs and Kisses" in packaged satin blanket-binding.

When constructing a quilt for a baby or child, remember back to your early days and identify your likes: coziness, warmth, flannel, satin, pink, purple, flowers. You may discover your tastes have changed, but remember, this quilt is not for you. Find your inner child and have fun with colors and designs you wouldn't usually choose. Playful quilts like this one might even lead you to new color combinations worth exploring in future projects.

Kelsey is enjoying herself at Mom's dressing table with a lipstick gift from Grandma Doodle. One of the joys of being a little girl these days is getting a new beauty product! As an extra touch, in a gift for a young woman, enclose a small fragrance package that color coordinates with the quilt.

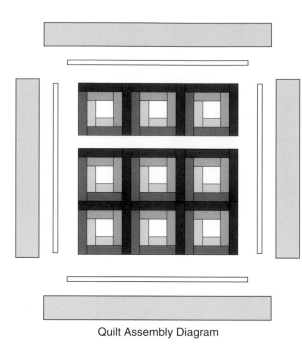

Quilt Assembly Diagram

Hugs and Kisses

DESIGNED BY:
Jackie Quinn

QUILTED BY:
Annette Harris

Finished quilt size:
37" x 37"

Finished block size:
9" x 9"

MATERIALS

Fabric requirements are based on 40" fabric width.

	Yardage	Cut
¼ yd.	Multicolor plaid for block centers	9 squares, 3½" x 3½"
½ yd.	Pink plaid for blocks and inner border	3 strips, 2" x 40" 4 border strips, 1¼" x 40"*
⅓ yd.	Blue plaid for blocks	4 strips, 2" x 40"
½ yd.	Red toile for blocks	5 strips, 2" x 40"
½ yd.	Blue toile for blocks	6 strips, 2" x 40"
¾ yd.	Floral print for outer border	4 border strips, 4½" x 40"*
2⅔ yds.**	Backing	
1 pkg.	(4¾ yds.) Satin blanket binding	
41" x 41"	Batting	

* Strips are cut longer than necessary, and will be trimmed to size later.

** If you don't mind working with a smaller-than-usual margin of backing fabric in your "quilt sandwich," it's possible to get the backing out of one length (rather than two) of 44-45"-wide fabric. In that case, you'll need 1⅜ yds. backing fabric.

DIRECTIONS

See *Basic Quiltmaking*, beginning on page 5, for general quiltmaking directions.

Block Assembly

1. Sew 9 multicolor plaid squares to 2"-wide pink plaid strip as shown, leaving a small space between each square. Cut units apart, trimming the strip edges even with each square. Press seams toward strip.

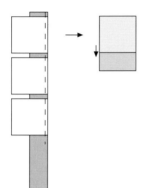

2. Sew units from Step 1 to remaining 2"-wide pink plaid strips, being sure to orient pieces as shown. Trim units; press seams toward strip.

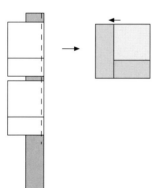

3. Sew units from Step 2 to blue plaid strips. Trim units; press seams toward strip.

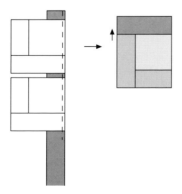

4. Using same technique as above, and referring to photo on page 43 for fabric placement, continue to sew units to strips. After adding a second blue plaid strip to each block, add red toile strips, followed by blue toile strips. Continue to press seams away from center of block.

Make 9.

5. Sew blocks in horizontal rows, then sew rows together as shown in the Quilt Assembly Diagram on page 44. Press for opposing seams (see page 8).

Border

1. Measure length of quilt top through center. Trim 2 of the pink plaid border strips to this measurement, and sew to sides of quilt. Press seams toward border.
2. Measure width of quilt top, including borders just added, through center. Trim the remaining 2 pink plaid border strips to this measurement, and sew to top and bottom of quilt. Press seams toward border.
3. Following general instructions in Steps 1 and 2 above, measure, trim, and sew floral border strips. Add side borders first, then top and bottom borders. Press seams toward border.

Finishing

1. Cut the backing fabric into two equal lengths and sew long edges together. Press seam open. Trim backing to 45" x 45".
2. Plan and mark quilting design as desired.
3. Layer quilt top, batting, and backing. Baste layers together.
4. Quilt by hand or machine.
5. Trim the batting and backing even with the quilt top edges.
6. Using satin blanket binding, bind the quilt edges the same as you would with regular binding (see page 11). Sew the two finished edges of the binding to front of quilt, and hand-stitch the folded edge of binding to back of quilt.
7. Add a hanging sleeve if desired. Sign and date your finished quilt.

My Home is My Castle

As Wendy designed this quilt, she remembered a favorite picture book from her childhood. The book showed children from all over the world, living in different types of housing, ranging from igloos to city apartments to grass huts. Wendy wanted to live in them all! Every once in a while she thought a castle might be nice, and since her family's duplex in Illinois didn't quite fit the bill, she built an imaginary castle under the dining room table.

She draped quilts for walls, and made a blue blanket moat to keep out intruders. Tip to parents: moms and dads bearing goodies are usually given a secret password and allowed to visit!

Can Daddy play too? While babies wave from windows in the quilt above, Zachary happily accepts a bribe from dad Jason.

MATERIALS

Fabric requirements are based on 40" fabric width.

Templates B, C, D, and E are on page 51. For instructions on using templates, see page 7.

		Yardage	Cut
⅔ yd. *total*		Assortment of blue prints for sky	For *each* house, cut: 2 Piece A, 2" x 3" 2 Template C and 2 Template C (*reversed*) 1 Template E and 1 Template E (*reversed*)
¼ yd. *total*		Assortment of green prints for grass	For *each* house, cut: 1 Piece O, 1½" x 9½"
1 yd. *total*		Assortment of bright pastel prints for castle walls	For *each* house, cut: 2 Piece F, 3½" x 4¼" 1 Piece G, 1" x 2" 1 Piece H, 1½" x 2" 4 Piece I, 5½" x 1½" 2 Piece J, 1½" x 2" 1 Piece K, 2" x 2½" 2 Piece L, 3" x 2"
½ yd. *total*		Assortment of geometric prints for roofs	For *each* house, cut: 2 Template B 1 Template D
¼ yd. *total*		Assortment of blue prints for windows	For *each* house, cut: 3 Piece N, 2" x 2"
¼ yd. *total*		Assortment of lavender/pink prints for doors	For *each* house, cut: 1 Piece M, 4" x 2½"
¼ yd.		Yellow print for inner border	4 strips, 1½" x 40"*
2 yds.		Blue print for outer border and binding	*Cut pieces in order given.* 5 widthwise binding strips, 2½" x 40" 4 lengthwise border strips, 5½" x 50"*
3⅓ yds.		Backing	
43½" x 52½"		Batting	

House Block

* Strips are cut longer than necessary, and will be trimmed to size later.

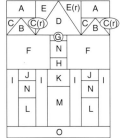

Quilt Assembly Diagram

My Home is My Castle

DESIGNED BY:
Wendy Slotboom

QUILTED BY:
Sherry D. Rogers

Finished quilt size:
39½" x 48½"

Finished block size:
9" x 12"

DIRECTIONS

See *Basic Quiltmaking*, beginning on page 5, for general quiltmaking directions.

Assembly

1. Assemble Castle pieces in rows as shown. Then sew rows together. Press seams in direction of arrows.

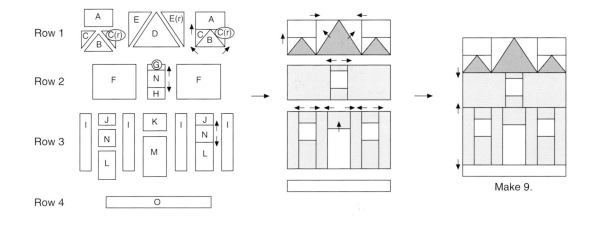

Make 9.

Tip:

1. For easy assembly of the sky and roof pieces, trim the points as marked on Templates B, C, D, and E.

2. Follow diagrams below to add sky pieces C and C(r) to roof piece B; and sky pieces E and E(r) to roof piece D. Press seams away from B and D pieces.

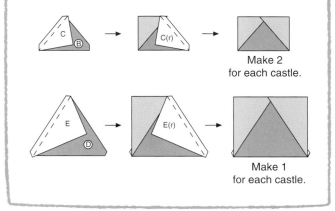

Make 2
for each castle.

Make 1
for each castle.

2. Sew blocks together in horizontal rows, then sew rows together as shown in the Quilt Assembly Diagram on page 49. Press for opposing seams (see page 8).

Borders

1. Measure length of quilt top through center. Trim 2 of the yellow border strips to this measurement, and sew to sides of quilt. Press seams toward border.

2. Measure width of quilt top, including borders just added, through center. Trim the remaining 2 yellow border strips to this measurement, and sew to top and bottom of quilt. Press seams toward border.

3. Following general instructions in Steps 1 and 2 above, measure, trim, and sew blue border strips. Add side borders first, then top and bottom borders. Press seams toward border.

Finishing

1. Cut the backing fabric into two equal lengths and sew long edges together. Press seam open. Trim backing to 47½" x 56½".

2. Plan and mark quilting design as desired.

3. Layer quilt top, batting, and backing. Baste layers together.

4. Quilt by hand or machine.

5. Trim the batting and backing even with the quilt top edges.

6. Sew the binding strips together to create one long strip. Bind the quilt edges.

7. Add a hanging sleeve if desired. Sign and date your finished quilt.

TEMPLATES

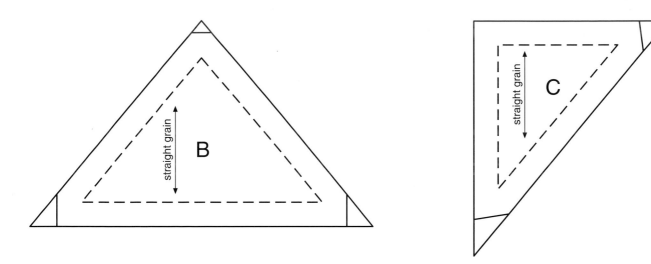

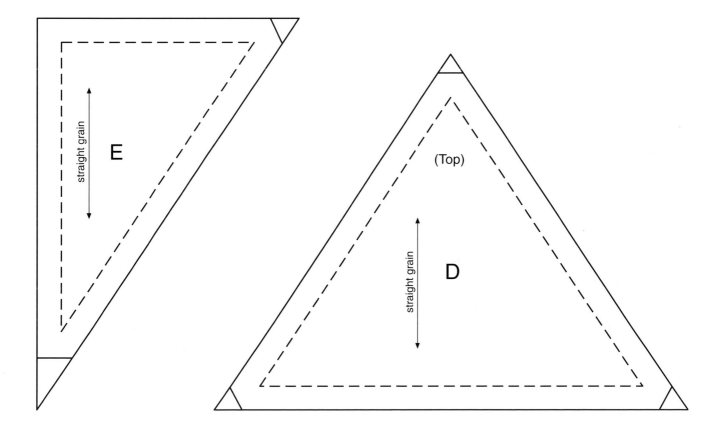

Sailor Jack

In making baby quilts for this book, many of us looked back to our own childhoods, and thought about the people who were most important to us as we were growing up. Margy named her quilt in honor of her father, Jack, who sailed with the merchant marines after serving in World War II. She chose the traditional Jack-in-the-Box block, and then picked a bright red sailor print for one of her two main fabrics. Margy kept her quilt simple with a straight set and no borders, then made sure that the design was visually exciting by alternating the placement of her red and yellow prints.

Young Connor has decided he'd like to go out to sea as the captain of his own yacht and be a television star on the "Adventures of Captain Connor." In the meantime, he's Captain of the family flower garden, and the closest he comes to water is by way of garden hose and watering can! Good job, Connor!

Quilt Assembly Diagram

Sailor Jack

DESIGNED BY:
Margy Duncan

QUILTED BY:
Margy Duncan

Finished quilt size:
38½" x 48"

Finished block size:
9½" x 9½"

MATERIALS

Fabric requirements are based on 40" fabric width.

	Yardage	Cut
1⅔ yds.	Red print for blocks	160 squares, 2⅞" x 2⅞" 40 rectangles, 2" x 4½"
1⅔ yds.	Yellow print for blocks	160 squares, 2⅞" x 2⅞" 40 rectangles, 2" x 4½"
⅝ yd.	Blue plaid for blocks and binding	20 squares, 2" x 2" 5 binding strips, 2½" x 40"
3⅓ yds.*	Backing	
42½" x 52"	Batting	

* If you don't mind working with a smaller-than-usual margin of backing fabric in your "quilt sandwich," it's possible to get the backing out of one length (rather than two) of 44-45"-wide fabric. In that case, you'll need 1¾ yds. backing fabric.

DIRECTIONS

See *Basic Quiltmaking,* beginning on page 5, for general quiltmaking directions.

Block Assembly

1. Using a ruler and sharp pencil, draw a diagonal line, from corner to corner, on the wrong side of all the yellow squares.

2. With right sides together, place a yellow square on top of a red square. Sew ¼" on each side of drawn line. Cut on drawn line. Open squares and press seams toward red fabric.

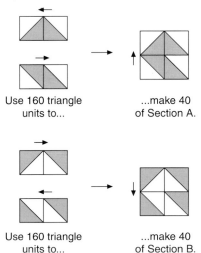

Make 320.

3. Sew triangle units together as shown, paying careful attention to color placement. Press seams in direction of arrows. (Pressing seams exactly as shown will make make blocks fit together easily in Step 5.)

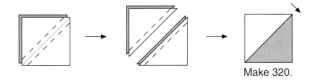

Use 160 triangle units to...   ...make 40 of Section A.

Use 160 triangle units to...   ...make 40 of Section B.

4. Using Sections A and B from Step 3, red rectangles, yellow rectangles, and blue plaid squares, assemble Jack-in-the-Box blocks as shown.

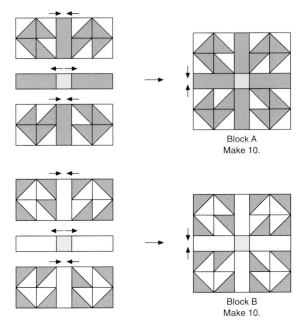

Block A
Make 10.

Block B
Make 10.

5. Sew blocks together in horizontal rows, then join rows together as shown in the Quilt Assembly Diagram on page 54. Press for opposing seams (see page 8).

Finishing

1. Cut the backing fabric into two equal lengths and sew long edges together. Press seam open. Trim backing to 46½" x 56".
2. Plan and mark quilting design as desired.
3. Layer quilt top, batting, and backing. Baste layers together.
4. Quilt by hand or machine.
5. Trim the batting and backing even with the quilt top edges.
6. Sew the binding strips together to create one long strip. Bind the quilt edges.
7. Add a hanging sleeve if desired. Sign and date your finished quilt.

Buckaroo Babies

One of Mary Jo's first quilting memories is of seeing Sunbonnet Sue and Irish Chain quilts at her Grandmother Josephine's house. These were lovely Depression era quilts made by Josephine, her mother, and sisters. Mary Jo is the proud owner of one of those Irish Chain quilts and credits her grandmother with inspiring her own love of sewing and quiltmaking.

Much of the fun of making quilts involves the giving and sharing of our love of quilts with others. Last year when In The Beginning CPA Julie Larsen announced she was expecting, Mary Jo was the first to offer to make a quilt for the new arrival. While the quilt was in the works, Julie discovered she was having twins! Hello, identical quilt number two. A satisfied Mary Jo finished the quilts and presented them to Julie. The gifts were received with much admiration and laughs for the western motifs, buckeroos, and cowgirls. A downcast member of the group was 4-year-old big brother Dylan, who considers himself an experienced cowboy ready to initiate little Connor and Katie into the ways of the West. Hello, identical quilt number three and a happy Dylan!

Little gifts (a pillow or pillowcase perhaps) made from scraps of your project are always a welcome surprise for big brothers and sisters!

Connor and Katie are all dressed up and rarin' to go on a buckaroo adventure. Saddle 'em up, because the twins are ready to ride.

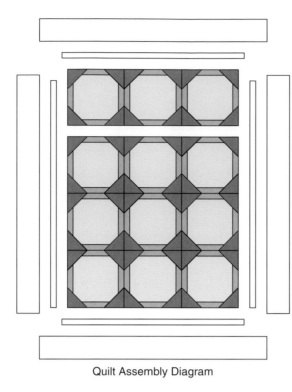

Quilt Assembly Diagram

Buckaroo Babies

DESIGNED BY:
Mary Jo Sisley

QUILTED BY:
Kathy Staley

Finished quilt size:
40½" x 50½"

Finished block size:
10" x 10"

MATERIALS

Fabric requirements are based on 40" fabric width.

	Yardage	Cut
1¼ yds.*	Large focal print for center of blocks	12 squares, 8½" x 8½"
¾ yd.	Yellow tone-on-tone for border of blocks	24 rectangles, 1½" x 8½" 24 rectangles, 1½" x 10½"
½ yd.	Small blue print for corners of blocks	24 squares, 4" x 4"
½ yd.	Red/white check for corners of blocks	24 squares, 4" x 4"
⅜ yd.	Red bandana print for inner border	5 strips, 1½" x 40"
1¾ yds.	Blue bandana print for outer border and binding	*Cut pieces in order given.* 5 widthwise binding strips, 2½" x 40" 4 lengthwise border strips, 4½" x 44"**
3½ yds.	Backing	
44½" x 54½"	Batting	

* Yardage is generous to allow for selective cutting of motifs.
** Strips are cut longer than necessary, and will be trimmed to size later.

DIRECTIONS

See *Basic Quiltmaking*, beginning on page 5, for general quiltmaking directions.

Block Assembly

1. Sew 8½" and 10½" yellow rectangles to sides of 8½" focal square as shown. Press seams toward rectangles.

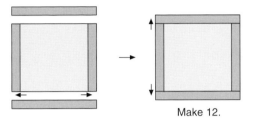

Make 12.

2. Using a ruler and sharp pencil, draw a diagonal line, from corner to corner, on the wrong side of all the 4" blue squares and 4" red/white squares.

3. With right sides together, place 2 blue squares on opposite diagonal corners of a block as shown. Sew on drawn line. Trim as shown, leaving a ¼" seam allowance. Press seams toward triangles.

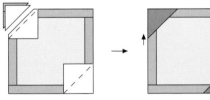

Make 12.

4. Using same technique as in Step 3: place, sew, and trim 2 red/white squares. Press seams toward triangles.

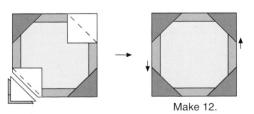

Make 12.

5. Sew blocks in horizontal rows; then sew rows together as shown in the Quilt Assembly Diagram on page 58. Press for opposing seams (see page 8).

Border

1. Sew 3 of the red bandana strips together, end-to-end, to make one long strip.

2. Measure length of quilt top through center. From the long strip, cut 2 border strips to this measurement, and sew to sides of quilt. Press seams toward border.

3. Measure width of quilt top, including borders just added, through center. Trim the remaining 2 red bandana border strips to this measurement, and sew to top and bottom of quilt. Press seams toward border.

4. Following general instructions in Steps 2 and 3 above, measure, trim, and sew blue bandana border strips. Add side borders first, then top and bottom borders. Press seams toward border.

Finishing

1. Cut the backing fabric into two equal lengths and sew long edges together. Press seam open. Trim backing to 48½" x 58½".

2. Plan and mark quilting design as desired.

3. Layer quilt top, batting, and backing. Baste layers together.

4. Quilt by hand or machine.

5. Trim the batting and backing even with the quilt top edges.

6. Sew the binding strips together to create one long strip. Bind the quilt edges.

7. Add a hanging sleeve if desired. Sign and date your finished quilt.

Rows of Bows

Wendy designed this charming quilt especially for girls. Fixed in her memory are all the years when niece Michelle's favorite colors were pink, pink, and pink! With enough pink bows to satisfy even Michelle, this quilt is absolutely sweet wrapped around a tiny baby. As babies grow up, the quilt becomes a perfect backdrop for little girls' playtime adventures.

For moms and grandmas wanting to create treasured memories, consider giving a jar of buttons to your daughter or granddaughter…then spend happy hours together, as you help her sew buttons onto her quilt. (This idea is for a young girl. No buttons for baby!)

Remember the song that goes: "Let's go where they keep on wearing those rings and things and buttons and bows"? Kelsey and Emily have found the place. They followed Wendy's Bow quilt and discovered a treasure trove of hats, jewels, and gorgeous clothes. Can a girl have more fun than playing dress-up with a friend?

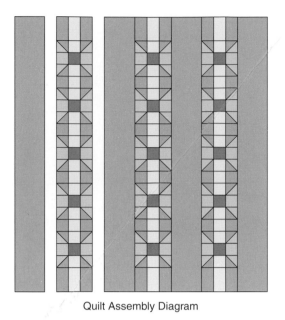

Quilt Assembly Diagram

Rows of Bows

DESIGNED BY:
Wendy Slotboom

QUILTED BY:
Wendy Slotboom

Finished quilt size:
38½" x 46½"

Finished block size:
6" x 6"

MATERIALS

Fabric requirements are based on 40" fabric width.

	Yardage	Cut
½ yd.	Light pink print for vertical ribbon	2 strips, 2½" x 40" 30 squares, 2½" x 2½"
¼ yd.	Dark pink print for centers of bows	2 strips, 2½" x 22"
½ yd.	Medium pink print #1 for bows	2 strips, 2½" x 22" 16 squares, 2⅞" x 2⅞"
½ yd.	Medium pink print #2 for bows	2 strips, 2½" x 22" 14 squares, 2⅞" x 2⅞"
2⅜ yds.	Blue tone-on-tone print for block background, vertical strips, and binding	*Cut pieces in order given.* 4 widthwise strips, 2½" x 40" 5 widthwise binding strips, 2½" x 40" 4 lengthwise strips, 5½" x 50"* 30 squares, 2⅞" x 2⅞"
3⅓ yds.**	Backing	
42½" x 50½"	Batting	

* Strips are cut longer than necessary, and will be trimmed to size later.

** If you don't mind working with a smaller-than-usual margin of backing fabric in your "quilt sandwich," it's possible to get the backing out of one length (rather than two) of 44-45"-wide fabric. In that case, you'll need 1⅔ yds. backing fabric.

DIRECTIONS

See *Basic Quiltmaking,* beginning on page 5, for general quiltmaking directions.

Block Assembly

1. Using 2 light pink and 4 blue tone-on-tone 2½" x 40" strips, make 2 strip units as shown. Press seams toward blue strips. From the strip units, cut 6 segments, each 4½" wide; and cut 12 segments, each 2½" wide.

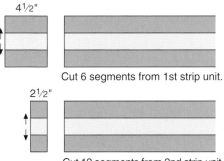

Cut 6 segments from 1st strip unit.

Cut 12 segments from 2nd strip unit.

2. Using the dark pink, medium pink #1, and medium pink #2 strips, make 2 strip units as shown. Press seams toward medium pink strips. From the medium pink #1 strip unit, cut 8 segments, each 2½" wide; from the medium pink #2 strip unit, cut 7 segments, each 2½" wide.

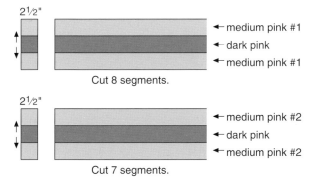

← medium pink #1
← dark pink
← medium pink #1

Cut 8 segments.

← medium pink #2
← dark pink
← medium pink #2

Cut 7 segments.

3. Using a ruler and sharp pencil, draw a diagonal line, from corner to corner, on the wrong side of all the medium pink #1 and medium pink #2 squares.

4. With right sides together, place a medium pink square on top of a blue tone-on-tone square. Sew ¼" on each side of drawn line. Cut on drawn line. Open squares and press seams toward blue fabric.

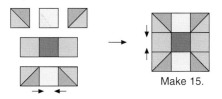

Make 60.

5. Using pink segments, triangle units, and light pink squares, assemble Bow block as shown. Press seams in direction of arrows.

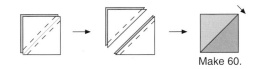

Make 15.

6. Sew Bow blocks, and blue/pink segments together in vertical rows as shown in the Quilt Assembly Diagram on page 62. Notice that the 4½" segments are placed at the top and bottom of each row.

7. Measure the length of each row (if they are slightly different, use the average length). Cut the 4 blue tone-on-tone lengthwise strips to this measurement, and sew together the rows and the blue strips. Press seams toward blue strips.

Finishing

1. Cut the backing fabric into two equal lengths and sew long edges together. Press seam open. Trim backing to 46½" x 54½".

2. Plan and mark quilting design as desired.

3. Layer quilt top, batting, and backing. Baste layers together.

4. Quilt by hand or machine.

5. Trim the batting and backing even with the quilt top edges.

6. Sew the binding strips together to create one long strip. Bind the quilt edges.

7. Add a hanging sleeve if desired. Sign and date your finished quilt.

Zoo Time

Many years ago when a certain Daddy was a small boy, his mother took him to the San Diego Zoo. It was a special visit with Mom, Aunt Mary, and his perky cousin Molly. The pace was slow because the two women were deep in conversation punctuated by peals of laughter. The boy rolled his ball to keep the group moving.

Suddenly Molly was pulling on Aunt Mary's sleeve, afraid to interrupt but knowing it was necessary. She pointed at the sight of her tiny cousin following his ball and scampering merrily among the giant giraffes. The animals stepped aside gingerly and stared at their small friend as he continued to play. A quick retrieval by a zoo employee ended the fun to the relief of Mom. Sharon wonders if that space under the fence is still there!

Commemorating events on a quilt is always a charming way to bring back special memories and give meaning to your quilts.

Zachary seems to be saying, "Grandma, these animals aren't real, and the balls don't bounce. Can we go to the zoo?"

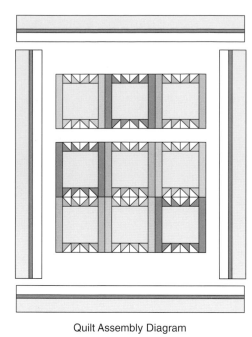

Quilt Assembly Diagram

Zoo Time

DESIGNED BY:
Sharon Yenter

QUILTED BY:
Sherry D. Rogers

Finished quilt size:
45" x 48"

Finished block size:
11" x 12"

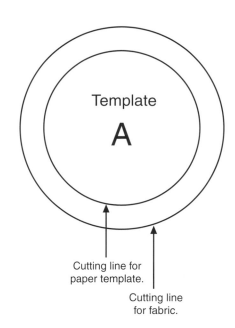

Cutting line for
paper template.

Cutting line
for fabric.

MATERIALS

Fabric requirements are based on 40" fabric width.

	Yardage	Cut
1 yd.	Animal panel print*	9 squares, 8½" x 8½"
⅜ yd.	Pink print for blocks and appliqué	12 squares, 2⅞" x 2⅞" 6 rectangles, 2" x 12½" 4 Template A *(use outer line for cutting)*
⅜ yd.	Green print for blocks and appliqué	12 squares, 2⅞" x 2⅞" 6 rectangles, 2" x 12½" 4 Template A *(use outer line for cutting)*
⅔ yd.	Purple print for blocks, appliqué, and second border	12 squares, 2⅞" x 2⅞" 6 rectangles, 2" x 12½" 4 Template A *(use outer line for cutting)* 6 border strips, 1¼" x 40"
⅞ yd.	White print for blocks and first border	36 squares, 2⅞" x 2⅞" 6 border strips, 2½" x 40"
1⅜ yds.	Multicolor stripe for outer border and binding	6 border strips, 3½" x 40" 2 squares, 18" x 18", to use for continuous bias binding *(see page 11)*
3⅓ yds.	Backing	
49" x 52"	Batting	

* Be sure to prewash fabric. The resulting shrinkage will square up the designs in the animal panel. Wash in warm
water and tumble dry on warm setting. Straighten animal panels by gently pulling diagonally and pressing.

DIRECTIONS

See *Basic Quiltmaking*, beginning on page 5, for general quiltmaking directions.

Block Assembly

1. Using a ruler and sharp pencil, draw a diagonal line, from corner to corner, on the wrong side of the white squares.

2. With right sides together, place a white square on top of a pink, green, or purple square. Sew ¼" on each side of drawn line. Cut on drawn line. Open squares and press seams toward darker fabric.

Make a total of 72 triangle units: 24 each of pink/white, green/white, and purple/white.

3. Sew like-colored triangle units together in rows as shown. Press seams open to reduce bulk.

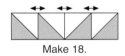

Make 18.

4. Referring to photo on page 65, sew animal squares, triangle rows, and 2" x 12½" rectangles together. Press seams in direction of arrows.

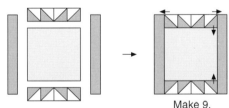

Make 9.

5. Sew blocks in horizontal rows; then sew rows together as shown in the Quilt Assembly Diagram on page 66. Press for opposing seams (see page 8).

Mitered Borders

1. Sewing along long sides, join together a white border strip, a purple border strip, and a stripe border strip. Press seams in one direction. Repeat to make a total of 6 of these border units.

Make 6.

Trim the ends to square up, then sew 3 border units together, end-to-end, in one long strip. Repeat to make a second long strip. From these long strips, cut 2 side border units, each 51" long; and 2 top and bottom border units, each 48" long.

2. With right sides together, center and sew 51"-long border units to sides of quilt top. Press seams toward borders. The borders will extend beyond the top and bottom of your quilt. Now center and sew the 48"-long border units to top and bottom of quilt; start and stop your seams at the point where the side borders join the quilt top. Miter corner by folding top border under at 45° angle as shown. Hand sew with an invisible stitch, then trim away excess, leaving a ¼" seam allowance. Repeat for each corner.

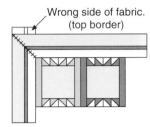

Wrong side of fabric. (top border)

Appliqué

1. Using the inside line of Template A (on page 66), cut 12 circle templates from heavy paper.
2. Stitching ⅛" from edge, hand-baste around each pink, green, and purple fabric circle. Don't tie off the tail of thread.
3. Center a paper template on the wrong side of each fabric circle. Pull the tail of basting thread to gather fabric around paper. Tie off thread. With hot iron, press circle firmly. After the fabric has cooled, remove the paper.

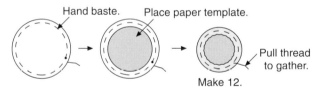

Hand baste. Place paper template. Pull thread to gather. Make 12.

4. Using a blind stitch, hand sew circles to quilt top. For placement guide, refer to photo on page 65.

Finishing

1. Cut the backing fabric into two equal lengths and sew long edges together. Press seam open. Trim backing to 53" x 56".
2. Plan and mark quilting design as desired.
3. Layer quilt top, batting, and backing. Baste layers together.
4. Quilt by hand or machine.
5. Trim the batting and backing even with the quilt top edges.
6. Bind the quilt edges with continuous bias binding (see page 11).
7. Add a hanging sleeve if desired. Sign and date your finished quilt.

Twinkling Stars

One of the perks of working in a quilt shop is getting to see all of the new fabrics as soon as they arrive. Some new prints are so appealing that they cause an acquisitive chain-reaction among the staff as everyone decides that they need a yard. Do any of us know what we're going to do with it? Of course not! We're just adding it to our stashes.

Then there's the fabric that In The Beginning produces. When the art arrives for the new lines, we gather around and "ooh" and "aah," and dream of the projects we'll make as soon as the fabric becomes reality.

When Wendy saw the art for designer Dena's fabric, she was immediately attracted to the blue colorway. Of course, she wanted the fabric *now*, but she, as well as everyone else, had to wait while the fabric was printed and shipped to Seattle.

Finally, it arrived! The prints were every bit as pretty as she had hoped and her finished quilt, with its soft blue tones, is perfectly suited to a child's quiet moments.

Jennifer takes a few minutes to relax with a colorful book in her special quilt corner. She likes using her quilt as "wall art" rather than bedding.

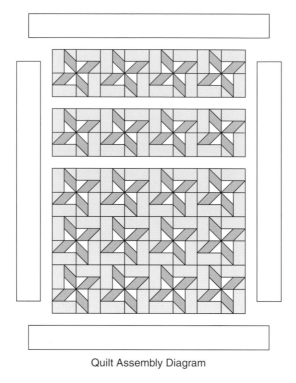

Quilt Assembly Diagram

Twinkling Stars

DESIGNED BY:
Wendy Slotboom

QUILTED BY:
Sherry D. Rogers

Finished quilt size:
40½" x 48½"

Finished block size:
8" x 8"

MATERIALS

Fabric requirements are based on 40" fabric width.

	Yardage	Cut
1¼ yds.	Light blue print for block background	80 rectangles, 2½" x 4½" 80 squares, 2½" x 2½"
1¼ yds.	Medium blue tone-on-tone for star points and binding	80 rectangles, 2½" x 4½" 5 binding strips, 2½" x 40"
½ yd.	White/blue print for pinwheel center of blocks	80 squares, 2½" x 2½"
1⅓ yds.	Blue dots on white for border	4 lengthwise strips, 4½" x 42"*
3⅓ yds.	Backing	
44½" x 52½"	Batting	

* Strips are cut longer than necessary, and will be trimmed to size later.

DIRECTIONS

See *Basic Quiltmaking*, beginning on page 5, for general quiltmaking directions.

Block Assembly

1. Using a ruler and sharp pencil, draw a diagonal line, from corner to corner, on the wrong side of all the light blue squares and white/blue squares.

2. With right sides together, place a white/blue square on a medium blue tone-on-tone rectangle as shown. Sew on drawn line. Trim excess, leaving a ¼" seam allowance. Press seam toward triangle.

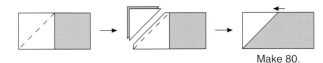

Make 80.

3. Using same technique as in Step 2: place, sew, and trim a light blue square. Press seam toward triangle.

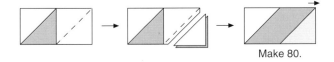

Make 80.

4. Sew unit from Step 3 to a light blue rectangle. Press seam toward rectangle.

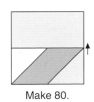

Make 80.

5. Assemble Twinkling Stars block as shown. Press seams open to reduce bulk.

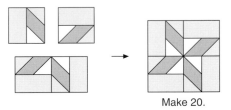

Make 20.

6. Sew blocks together in horizontal rows; then join rows as shown in the Quilt Assembly Diagram on page 70. Press seams open.

Border

1. Measure length of quilt top through center. Trim 2 of the border strips to this measurement, and sew to sides of quilt. Press seams toward border.
2. Measure width of quilt top, including borders just added, through center. Trim the remaining 2 border strips to this measurement, and sew to top and bottom of quilt. Press seams toward border.

Finishing

1. Cut the backing fabric into two equal lengths and sew long edges together. Press seam open. Trim backing to 48½" x 56½".
2. Plan and mark quilting design as desired.
3. Layer quilt top, batting, and backing. Baste layers together.
4. Quilt by hand or machine.
5. Trim the batting and backing even with the quilt top edges.
6. Sew the binding strips together to create one long strip. Bind the quilt edges.
7. Add a hanging sleeve if desired. Sign and date your finished quilt.

Little Guy

Laurie is a long distance aunt to four nephews and three nieces. Since Laurie isn't able to see them as often as she'd like, she shows her love through quilts. Each nephew and niece has (or will) receive three quilts from Aunt Laurie. One quilt for their baby and toddler years, one for their juvenile years, and one for their teenage years. Doing the math…that's 21 quilts!

For her "Little Guy" quilt, Laurie designed a quick project that can easily be made by new aunts or grandmothers embarking on their very first quiltmaking adventure. Pick three coordinating fabrics and you're on your way. The cutting is easy: squares, rectangles, and strips. After finishing this project, you may find yourself following Laurie's example…counting the babies in your family and multiplying by three quilts!

Tyler and Connor celebrate the completion of another quilt that will travel to the East Coast as a gift from Aunt Laurie. Are these buddies really toasting the quilt with their ice cream cones…or are they just gobbling down every bite?

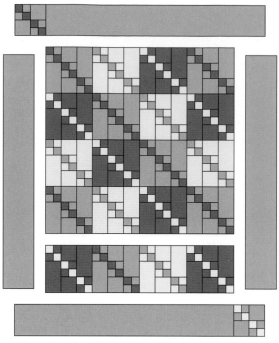

Quilt Assembly Diagram

Little Guy

DESIGNED BY:
Laurie Shifrin

QUILTED BY:
Laurie Shifrin

Finished quilt size:
40½" x 48"

Finished block size:
7½" x 7½"

MATERIALS

Fabric requirements are based on 40" fabric width.

	Yardage	Cut
1¾ yds.	Pastel batik with blue, pink, and yellow for blocks, border, and binding	5 strips, 1¾" x 40" 18 squares, 3" x 3" 14 rectangles, 3" x 5½" 2 border strips, 5½" x 38" 2 border strips, 5½" x 35½" 5 binding strips, 2½" x 40"
⅝ yd.	Yellow batik for blocks	4 strips, 1¾" x 40" 12 squares, 3" x 3" 12 rectangles, 3" x 5½"
¾ yd.	Teal tone-on-tone for blocks	5 strips, 1¾" x 40" 14 squares, 3" x 3" 14 rectangles, 3" x 5½"
3⅓ yds.	Backing	
44½" x 52"	Batting	

Pictured are Sharon Evans Yenter, owner of In The Beginning; son Jason, president; and grandson, Zack, cover boy and latest addition to the In The Beginning family.

Acknowledgments

As a new grandmother, this book was a natural. It was so much fun sharing stories, quilts, kids and babies with moms, dads, and proud grandparents.

A big thank you to all who were associated with this book, and double thanks to these folks:

Much of the credit for the book goes to Editor Wendy Slotboom, Toby's mom, and an extraordinary talent technically and creatively. It is difficult to find someone with right and left brain skills, but she magically combines both.

Barbara Schmitt manages to convey my vision wonderfully. Each book becomes what I initially pictured, and much more, because of her design skills.

Photographer Melanie Blair added beauty and wonder to her photos of childhood.

The staff members from In The Beginning, who are so talented and always willing to contribute. They have been my secret strength for 25 years.

Sherry D. Rogers and Kathy Staley, our wonderful quilters.

Trish Carey and Melissa McCulloch made scouting for props a fun exploration.

My son Jason, who runs In The Beginning splendidly so I can do the "really fun" stuff!

My wonderful family, especially husband Bill who is patient and understanding while I follow my obsession.

Author and Designers

Sharon Evans Yenter is the owner of In The Beginning Fabrics in Seattle, Washington. She is the author of *Floral Bouquet Quilts* and co-author of *Blended Quilts From In The Beginning*. During her 25 years as a shop owner, she has taught and designed patterns. She currently produces fabric for her own textile company.

Sharon is a longtime collector of antique quilts, sees herself as a caretaker of those quilts and is committed to spreading the history, art, friendship, and fun of quiltmaking.

She was assisted on this project by the talented staff at In The Beginning. Staff members contributed not just quilt designs, but also children, grandchildren, a cat, and various props. Add ice cream sundaes to the mix, and you have a photo shoot that will not soon be forgotten!

Credits

Editor: Wendy Slotboom

Technical Editor: Laurie Shifrin

Copy Editor: Gloria Young

Photography: Melanie Blair

Photo Styling:

Sharon Yenter, Trish Carey,

Melissa McCulloch and Barbara Schmitt

Art Direction and Design: Barbara Schmitt

Illustrations: Wendy Slotboom

Published by:

In The Beginning Fabrics

8201 Lake City Way N.E.

Seattle, WA 98115

206.523.6056

Kids

Thank you to all the great kids who came to the photo shoot and had fun with our quilts. You made this book sparkle as bright as your smiles!

Aleyah Bennett, Fiona Campbell, Kelsey Early, Kimberly Evans, Tyler Evans, Alicia Hernandez, Emily Hernandez, Connor Johnson, Cassandra Kerschner, Connor and Katie Larsen, Dylan Larsen, Jennifer Nelson, Toby Slotboom, Ruby Sylvester, Zachary Yenter.

Playtime to Bedtime Quilts from In The Beginning
© 2002 Sharon Evans Yenter
In The Beginning, Seattle, Washington USA

ISBN 0-970690029

Printed in Hong Kong

DIRECTIONS

See *Basic Quiltmaking*, beginning on page 5, for general quiltmaking directions.

Block Assembly

1. Using pastel batik, yellow batik, and teal strips (each 1¾" x 40"), make 7 strip units. Arrange colors as shown in diagrams. Press seams in direction of arrows. From the strip units, cut segments (see diagrams for amounts), each 1¾" wide.

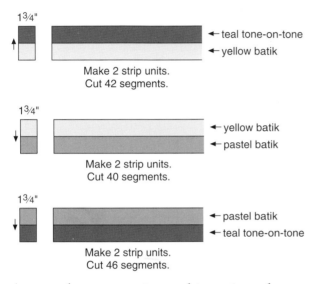

1¾"
← teal tone-on-tone
← yellow batik

Make 2 strip units.
Cut 42 segments.

1¾"
← yellow batik
← pastel batik

Make 2 strip units.
Cut 40 segments.

1¾"
← pastel batik
← teal tone-on-tone

Make 2 strip units.
Cut 46 segments.

2. Arrange the segments in matching pairs and sew together to make Fourpatch units. Press seams in one direction.

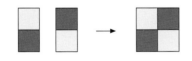

Make 21.
(teal and yellow)

Make 20.
(yellow and pastel)

Make 23.
(pastel and teal)

3. Using Fourpatch units, 3" squares, and 3" x 5½" rectangles, assemble blocks as shown. Study photo on page 73 and diagrams for correct color placement. Press seams in direction of arrows. Make 20 large blocks and 2 small blocks (for border).

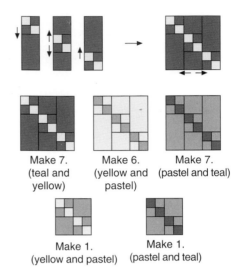

Make 7.
(teal and yellow)

Make 6.
(yellow and pastel)

Make 7.
(pastel and teal)

Make 1.
(yellow and pastel)

Make 1.
(pastel and teal)

4. Sew 20 large blocks together in horizontal rows; then sew rows together as shown in the Quilt Assembly Diagram on page 74. Press for opposing seams (see page 8).

Border

1. Sew 5½" x 38" border strips to sides of quilt top. Press seams toward border.
2. Sew 2 small blocks to ends of 5½" x 35½" border strips as shown in the Quilt Assembly Diagram. Press seams toward border strips. Sew these pieced strips to top and bottom of quilt. Press seams toward border.

Finishing

1. Cut the backing fabric into two equal lengths and sew long edges together. Press seam open. Trim backing to 48½" x 56".
2. Plan and mark quilting design as desired.
3. Layer quilt top, batting, and backing. Baste layers together.
4. Quilt by hand or machine.
5. Trim the batting and backing even with the quilt top edges.
6. Sew the binding strips together to create one long strip. Bind the quilt edges.
7. Add a hanging sleeve if desired. Sign and date your finished quilt.